Original title:
In the Land Beyond

Copyright © 2024 Creative Arts Management OÜ
All rights reserved.

Author: Gideon Shaw
ISBN HARDBACK: 978-9916-90-088-8
ISBN PAPERBACK: 978-9916-90-089-5

The Lost Lullabies of Distant Worlds

In twilight's glow, the stars do weep,
For lullabies that time can't keep,
Whispers from lands both far and near,
Echo in dreams, soft yet clear.

The moon sings low, its silver tune,
Of gardens blooming beneath the rune,
Where shadows dance on ancient stone,
Forgotten tales, now overgrown.

Through cosmic winds, a voice does call,
From hidden realms where wonders sprawl,
Each note a thread in the vast expanse,
A melody lost in a timeless dance.

In silence wrapped, we seek the past,
With every heartbeat, shadows cast,
Yet in the night, hope flickers bright,
As lost lullabies return to light.

Whispers of the Forgotten Terrain

In the heart of a quiet grove,
Secrets rustle in the leaves.
Footsteps soft on mossy paths,
Ancient stories the forest weaves.

Moonlight glimmers on still streams,
Casting shadows, cool and clear.
Whispers ride the evening breeze,
Echoing what we long to hear.

Among the ferns where spirits play,
Time stands still in its embrace.
Each moment lingers, holds its breath,
In nature's tender, sacred space.

Shadows Dance on Distant Shores

Waves crash softly on the sand,
While twilight paints the skies.
Whispers float on salty air,
In the glow where silence lies.

Footprints lead to where we dream,
Underneath the starry veil.
The horizon blushes crimson,
As evening takes the sail.

Dancing silhouettes embrace,
As night wraps all in grace.
Gentle hearts sway like the tide,
Lost in time, they find their place.

Echoes of the Untamed Horizon

Mountains rise with rugged pride,
Underneath a canvas vast.
Wild creatures roam the open fields,
Each moment rushing past.

Thunder rolls in distant realms,
A symphony of earth and sky.
Voices call through woods and winds,
In the place where eagles fly.

Every echo tells a tale,
Of journeys woven deep in air.
Threads of fate entwined with dreams,
In whispers, worlds laid bare.

Dreams on the Edge of Infinity

Stars shimmer on a velvet night,
As thoughts drift and take their flight.
Where time bends and heartbeats race,
In the shadows of eternal space.

Hopes unfurl like petals wide,
Each desire a fleeting ride.
In realms where possibilities blend,
Every moment whispers, 'mend'.

Across the void, we reach and sway,
In dreams that guide us on our way.
Chasing echoes in the dark,
Finding light within the spark.

Beyond the Silver Mist

Whispers float on silver air,
Where shadows dance with gentle care.
A realm where dreams begin to blend,
Among the clouds, our hearts ascend.

Beneath the moon's soft, tender glow,
The secrets of the night bestow.
In silent pools, reflections gleam,
Inviting souls to chase their dream.

Winds carry echoes of the past,
Through ancient trees, their spells are cast.
Each step reveals what lies in wait,
As wanderers embrace their fate.

Beyond this mist, the dawn does rise,
Unraveling truths beneath the skies.
With every breath, we start anew,
In worlds where wishes all come true.

Secrets of the Ethereal Plane

In twilight's hue, the spirit flies,
Where silence dwells and echoes rise.
Veils of light and shadow play,
Guarding secrets of the day.

Celestial paths, they intertwine,
Offering visions, pure and divine.
With every glance, the heart will race,
In this realm of time and space.

Here, thoughts are seeds that bloom and grow,
In gardens where lost whispers flow.
Each moment lingers, soft and clear,
As dreams unveil what we hold dear.

Embrace the night, let magic swell,
In this ethereal, sacred shell.
The secrets kept, so vast, so bright,
Guide us gently into the light.

The Enchanted Expanse

Beneath a sky of endless blue,
An expanse where wonders brew.
Each step reveals a dance so grand,
In lands where dreams and fate expand.

Mossy trails and crystal streams,
Awaken long-forgotten dreams.
Breezes sing through ancient trees,
In harmony with whispered pleas.

Colors swirl in vibrant tones,
Where every creature finds its home.
In twilight's glow, the tales emerge,
Of journeys taken, souls that surge.

The heart embraces nature's grace,
In this enchanted, sacred space.
Each moment shared, a precious gift,
In the expanse where spirits drift.

Unlocking the Hidden Gates

A door concealed, with stories untold,
Awaits the brave, the young, the old.
With whispered key and hopeful hand,
The heart shall guide, as fate has planned.

Beyond the wood and ancient stone,
Lies realms where seeds of thought are sown.
The magic sings in every crack,
As souls unite, there's no turning back.

Each gate unlocks a timeless frame,
With echoes soft, they'll call your name.
Through every threshold, wonders wait,
To guide you on to destiny's gate.

Step forth with courage, take the leap,
Into the promises you keep.
For in these gates, the world expands,
Unlocking truths held in your hands.

The Tides of Ancient Whispers

In shadows deep, where echoes play,
The whispers of time gently sway.
Old tales carried on the breeze,
Secrets locked in ancient trees.

Waves collide with the shore's embrace,
Each tide tells a forgotten space.
Boats adrift on a silver sea,
Searching for what used to be.

Moonlight dances on water's glass,
Illuminating moments that pass.
A chorus of stars sings so bright,
Guiding lost souls through the night.

Beneath the Canopy of Dreams

Layers high, the leaves entwine,
Whispers soft, where hopes align.
Crickets sing in the warm night's air,
Dreams unfurling without a care.

Stars peek through with silver eyes,
Lighting paths where the heart flies.
In the stillness, magic brews,
Spirits dance, the night renews.

Branches sway with a gentle grace,
Inviting all to find their place.
Beneath the canopy, souls merge,
In the night's soft, embracing surge.

Reverie in the Twilight Grove

Twilight falls in hues of gold,
Casting dreams both soft and bold.
In the grove where shadows meet,
Magic lingers at our feet.

Whispers float on the evening air,
Stories woven, pure and rare.
Fireflies blink with curious light,
Guiding hearts through the night.

Timeless secrets linger still,
As the world begins to thrill.
In reverie, we softly tread,
Awakening the dreams we've fed.

The Quest for the Hidden Oasis

Amidst the sands, where silence reigns,
A hidden haven calls our names.
With every step, the pulse ignites,
Whispers of hope in the desert nights.

Mirages dance, elusive and bright,
Guiding travelers lost in their plight.
But a heart that seeks will surely find,
The oasis where dreams unwind.

Water flows with a gentle grace,
Mirroring the sun's warm embrace.
In this refuge, all fears cease,
And souls are cradled in sweet peace.

Voices from the Astral Fields

Whispers drift on cosmic breeze,
Carried far through starlit seas.
Shadows dance with spectral grace,
In the void, we find our place.

Echoes of a time long past,
Fleeting dreams, a spell that's cast.
Murmurs weave through night's embrace,
Guiding souls to quiet space.

Celestial songs entwine with fate,
Universal threads we cultivate.
In silence, learn what stars reveal,
Hidden truths that softly heal.

Songs of light, a heavenly call,
Lifting spirits, uniting all.
From astral fields, we find our way,
Voices guide us, night or day.

Retreat to the Fringes of Dreams

Fleeting visions blur and blend,
In the night, where shadows bend.
Wandering paths through realms unseen,
Where reality meets the serene.

Lanterns flicker with gentle glow,
In the corners where secrets flow.
Whispers brush against the mind,
Echoes of what we seek to find.

Through the veil, we softly tread,
Into landscapes of silver thread.
Daring to stretch beyond the sane,
To embrace both joy and pain.

In dreams' cradle, we take flight,
Escaping into velvet night.
Fringes of slumber call us near,
Home awaits, where all is clear.

The Path of Ancient Echoes

Footsteps trace the dusty road,
Through the tales of ages flowed.
Ancient voices guide our way,
Lessons learned from yesterday.

Rivers whisper of the time,
As they flow with purpose, rhyme.
Nature's secrets softly share,
Wisdom found in every stare.

From the hills, the stories rise,
Carrying dreams that touch the skies.
Each stone holds a fractured tale,
Of those who dared to set the sail.

In the twilight, shadows play,
Resting in the dusk of day.
The echoes call, we shall not part,
For ancient paths are close to heart.

Echoes in the Mysterious Fog

Veils of mist shroud the dawn,
In the hush, the world is drawn.
Silence swells with secrets bare,
Mysterious whispers fill the air.

Shadows linger, softly creep,
Guarding dreams that dare to sleep.
Footfalls lost in twilight haze,
Guide us through the secret maze.

Voices murmur, lost in time,
Every note a haunting rhyme.
Through the fog, the spirits sigh,
Ethereal songs that never die.

In the depths of muted light,
We awaken to the night.
Echoes dance among the trees,
Calling softly, on the breeze.

Floating Between Realities

In dreams we drift through veils so thin,
Where shadows dance and echoes begin.
A whisper of light, a flicker of night,
We wander through worlds, in search of insight.

Time bends and twists, as thoughts take flight,
Between the realms, we find our might.
In silence we float, a delicate thread,
Connected to all, where fears are shed.

Holding our breath, we leap once more,
Into the unknown, a vast open door.
With each heartbeat, the cosmos aligns,
Floating through spaces where the mystic shines.

Here we discover that all is one,
In the cosmic dance, we become the sun.
Between the realities, we learn to see,
The beauty in chaos, the calm in the sea.

Stars That Never Set

In the velvet sky, our wishes soar,
Stars twinkle softly, forever more.
They light our dreams, a guiding spark,
Shining through shadows, igniting the dark.

Each pinprick of hope, a story untold,
Of love and laughter, of brave and bold.
They twine through the night, with grace divine,
Stars that never set, eternally shine.

Boundless horizons, where night meets day,
Whispers of secrets in the Milky Way.
In the silence, they sing, a celestial tune,
Revealing the mystery of sun and moon.

Under the canopy, our hearts entwine,
Together we bask in the cosmic design.
With stars as our witness, we take a stand,
In a universe vast, forever hand in hand.

The Realm Where Time Stands Still

In the quiet hush, where moments freeze,
We find the stillness in the whispering trees.
Time loses meaning, flows like a stream,
In this sacred place, we can only dream.

The sun hangs low, in a painted sky,
Where echoes of laughter and beauty shy.
In shadows of twilight, possibilities blend,
In the realm where time has no end.

With every heartbeat, we drift and sway,
In the arms of eternity, we find our way.
New beginnings blossom, like flowers in spring,
In the stillness, we learn what love can bring.

Here, past and future become a single thread,
In the realm of now, we move ahead.
Tranquility whispers, like a gentle thrill,
In the magic of moments where time stands still.

Songs of the Invisible Journey

We walk a path that's seldom seen,
In shadows and light, where we convene.
With every footstep, a story unfolds,
Echoes of wisdom in whispers bold.

Through valleys of doubt, and mountains of grace,
We seek the signs in each hidden space.
With hearts as our compass, we find our way,
In songs of the journey, both night and day.

Though unseen they are, the melodies play,
Guiding our spirits with love on display.
An invisible dance, in perfect time,
The rhythm of life, a celestial rhyme.

So let us embark on this winding road,
With dreams as our lanterns, lightening the load.
In songs of the journey, we sing our truth,
Connecting all hearts, igniting our youth.

Chronicles of an Unknown Wilderness

In the silence of the trees,
Whispers of the ancient breeze,
Footsteps tread on hidden stones,
Echoes linger, all alone.

Branches arch in twisted grace,
Shadows dance in dimmed embrace,
Secrets woven in the night,
Stars above, a flickered light.

Rivers carve through rugged land,
Nature's artistry so grand,
A path lost yet found anew,
Wilderness calls, wild and true.

Time unravels in this space,
Every moment leaves a trace,
Chronicles of life unfold,
In this tale, the brave and bold.

The Otherworldly Embrace

In twilight's gentle, glowing hue,
Veils of mystery drift anew,
A realm where dreams and shadows blend,
Where time and space quietly suspend.

Softly hum the stars above,
Whispers of an ethereal love,
Caressing winds that call my name,
A dance of souls, their spirits tame.

In this place, beyond the real,
Hearts entwined, our fates congeal,
With every breath, the universe sways,
In the otherworldly, forever stays.

Embrace the magic, let it flow,
In realms where only dreamers go,
Together we will soar unchained,
In our hearts, the endless gained.

Dreams from the Edge of Existence

On the brink where shadows meet,
Whispers rise on agile feet,
Visions swirl in fragile air,
A tapestry of dreams laid bare.

Fleeting moments, time suspended,
In the silence, thoughts extended,
Awake to depths of hidden fears,
Reality blurs; all disappears.

Within the chasm of the mind,
Wander lost, yet seek to find,
An echo of what once was true,
The edge of life that greets the view.

Dreams drift softly, then depart,
Leaving traces on the heart,
In this space of endless night,
Existence glimmers, purest light.

A Tapestry of Celestial Threads

Woven within the starlit sky,
Galaxies twist as comets fly,
Threads of silver, gold, and blue,
We connect as the cosmos do.

Each star a tale of ages passed,
In the fabric, moments cast,
Fates entwined by unseen hands,
In the great expanse, all life stands.

Nebulas cradle whispers sweet,
In the dawn where worlds all meet,
A tapestry of dreams is spun,
Under the gaze of the endless sun.

Life's patterns dance, yet remain,
In the joy, in the pain,
Celestial threads, so intertwined,
In this woven space, love binds.

Flickering Lights of Distant Realms

Stars twinkle far, a silent show,
Whispers of worlds we long to know.
Shadows dance in celestial flight,
Guiding dreams through the velvet night.

Galaxies swirl in cosmic embrace,
Each flicker a voice, a timeless trace.
Across the void, we seek to soar,
In the glow of what we can't ignore.

Wonders beckon from beyond the haze,
In the depths of night, we lose our gaze.
A tapestry woven in starlit threads,
Where hopes awaken and silence spreads.

Beneath this dome, our spirits rise,
Chasing the light through endless skies.
Flickering dreams in realms unknown,
Connected by light, yet all alone.

Serpents of Smoke and Allure

In shadows deep, the whispers curl,
Serpents of smoke in a secret whirl.
Elusive forms that twist and glide,
In their dance, we cannot hide.

With charms of night, they beckon near,
Veils of mystery, cloaked in fear.
Seductive trails through the stillness flow,
Guiding hearts where no one goes.

Mirrored reflections in the haze,
Lost in the labyrinth of smoky ways.
Captivated, we lean to see,
What lies beneath the mystic plea.

In the heart of dusk, where secrets play,
Time unfolds in a serpentine way.
Allure of smoke, both thick and light,
Serpents of dreams that haunt the night.

Inscriptions of Cosmic Dust

Across the void, a canvas vast,
Inscriptions of dust from ages past.
Each grain tells tales of time and space,
Whispers of life in the universe's embrace.

Fleeting moments in stardust spun,
Echoes of battles, lost and won.
Galaxies rise, and in their wake,
Stories inscribed for the dreamer's sake.

From nebulae bright to comets' trails,
Scribbled in silence, the cosmos exhales.
In every shimmer, a history swirls,
A dance of creation as mystery unfurls.

We chase the light and heed the call,
Seeking the wonders that bind us all.
In every spark, a truth we trust,
Eternal whispers in cosmic dust.

The Breath of Eternal Meadows

Beneath the sky where wildflowers sway,
The breath of meadows invites us to stay.
Soft whispers carried on the breeze,
Nature's lullaby through ancient trees.

Fields of gold stretch far and wide,
Stories of time in the sun's warm glide.
Each rustling blade a gentle sigh,
Connecting earth and the endless sky.

Moments linger in the fragrant air,
Embraced by peace, free from despair.
The heart finds solace in nature's light,
Guided by wonder, our spirits take flight.

In twilight's glow, a world reborn,
The breath of meadows, a soothing adorn.
In every heartbeat, love's gentle thread,
Weaving our lives where beauty is spread.

Whispers from the Celestial Shore

Stars twinkle softly in the dark,
Gentle waves kiss the silver sand.
Whispers drift on the cool night air,
Carried far by the moon's command.

Drifting thoughts like clouds do flow,
Light entwined with shimmering dreams.
Each breath taken, a fleeting glow,
Guiding hearts through celestial beams.

Echoes of love from realms above,
Wrapped in mystery, softly they call.
As night unfolds, we find our place,
In this dance, we surrender all.

With every whisper, the silence sings,
A lullaby from the ethereal sea.
Where souls connect and laughter rings,
At the shore where we long to be.

Shadows of the Eternal Night

The shadows stretch beneath the trees,
Whispers quiet in the haunted air.
Echoes linger with each cold breeze,
Memories woven with tender care.

Silhouettes dance in the ghostly light,
Stories hidden in the fading past.
In the embrace of the endless night,
We find the truths that ever last.

Flickering flames trace ancient tales,
Of love and loss beneath the stars.
Through every struggle, the heart prevails,
Facing the darkness, we find our scars.

In this realm where the lost reside,
Hope flickers like a distant flame.
Shadows not feared, but held inside,
Guide us softly, like an old name.

Navigating the Dreamscape

In the realm where dreams take flight,
Visions weave through twilight haze.
Whispers soft as the stars ignite,
Leading us through the moonlit maze.

Fragments glimmer, the mind's delight,
Every thought a luminous thread.
Floating free on the edge of night,
Where the conscious and dreamers tread.

Journey forth on a starlit stream,
Through valleys deep and mountains grand.
In this dance of the waking dream,
We discover what is truly planned.

With eyes wide open, we chase the light,
Embracing all that the heart can hold.
Navigating through shadows and bright,
In the dreamscape, we become bold.

A Dance with the Unfathomable

In the depths of the cosmic sea,
We twirl with the unknown divine.
With every heartbeat, we are free,
Embracing stars that weave and shine.

Gravity lost in the swirling space,
Holding hands with the undefined.
In this dance, we find our grace,
Threading the fabric of time entwined.

Each step whispers of ancient lore,
As we glide through the endless night.
In the vastness, we seek for more,
Exploring realms bathed in soft light.

With every moment, the shadows play,
Unfathomable truths unfold.
In this dance, we find a way,
To weave together the brave and bold.

The Secret Gardens of Vague Realities

In whispered dreams where shadows play,
Petals dance in soft dismay.
Hidden paths of emerald hue,
A world awakes, yet feels askew.

Moonlight spills on secrets kept,
Where silent sighs and echoes swept.
Winds of change through babbling brooks,
In each glance, a thousand books.

Time slips by in forgotten glades,
With gentle hands, the vision fades.
Yet still the blooms of hope arise,
Transforming dark to endless skies.

In every corner lies a spark,
Lost reveries in layers stark.
The heart beats true, though hushed by fear,
In gardens vast, the truth draws near.

A Window to the Infinite

Through glass so clear, a vision flows,
A universe where wonder grows.
Stars collide in whispered light,
Beyond the reach of day or night.

With every gaze, dimensions shift,
A silent gift, a cosmic drift.
What lies beyond the painted frame,
In boundless realms, we seek a name.

The edges blur, the colors blend,
A timeless dance that has no end.
We trace the lines of fate anew,
Through windows wide, our dreams break through.

In every glance, a spark ignites,
A journey toward celestial heights.
Between the worlds, we dare to leap,
Into the dreams that never sleep.

The Allure of the Unexplored

Each whispered path calls out to roam,
In secret places far from home.
The wild unknown, a siren's song,
Where fleeting hearts and passions throng.

Beneath the boughs of ancient trees,
Adventure drifts on summer breeze.
The shadows hold their myths and tales,
In every creak, a journey trails.

We dance on edges, thrill and fear,
To chase the echoes, bright and clear.
The heart beats loud, the compass spins,
In every loss, a chance to win.

With every turn, new wonders see,
The unexplored will set us free.
In every step, reminders spark,
That truth awaits in every arc.

Fragmented Journeys of Light

A flicker here, a glimmer there,
Fragments of dreams float in the air.
Each moment catches breaths and sighs,
In prisms cast from hidden skies.

The pathways wind in disarray,
But every twist leads us away.
To places bright yet dimly known,
Where seeds of thought have softly grown.

Radiant beams break through the dark,
In scattered glances, each a spark.
Lessons learned in fractured sights,
In the chaos, we find our lights.

With open hearts, we dare to seek,
The beauty found in every peak.
Through broken shards, our visions blend,
In journeys vast that never end.

Whims of the Celestial Waters

Whispers dance upon the waves,
Stars above in silver caves,
Moonlight bathes the rippling flow,
Secrets in the water's glow.

Ripples tell a tale untold,
Of dreams and wishes bright as gold,
In the depths, the truths reside,
By the shore, we must abide.

With each tide, the stories fade,
Yet the heartache will not trade,
In the swell, we lose and find,
Emotions deep, forever blind.

Celestial whimsy pulls the strings,
Creating joy, as laughter sings,
In the ebb and flow of night,
Water cradles pure delight.

The Tides of Forgotten Memories

Once lived moments, drifting past,
Tides that pull and hold us fast,
Faces fade in shadows deep,
While the ocean sings to sleep.

Faded photographs in hand,
Symbols of a fleeting land,
Echoes of what used to be,
Lost in time, like grains at sea.

Waves recede, but still they yearn,
For the lessons hard to learn,
Hopes and dreams wash on the shore,
To be cherished, held once more.

With each surf, the heart does ache,
Memories linger, softly break,
Yet in loss, we start to see,
Life's quiet beauty, endlessly.

Harmony in the Undefined

Shadows meld with beams of light,
Colors blend, a lovely sight,
In the chaos, find the tune,
Sunrise meets the brightening moon.

Lines are blurred, yet worlds collide,
In the fusion, we abide,
Notes that form a gentle breeze,
Whispers dancing through the trees.

Unexpected paths we tread,
Silent thoughts seem widely bred,
In the space where chaos reigns,
Peace is found in risk and gains.

Harmony lies in the unknown,
In the silence, seeds are sown,
With each step, we redefine,
Life's sweet song, both yours and mine.

Beyond the Obsidian Gates

In the dark, where secrets hide,
Mysteries waiting, filled with pride,
Gates of onyx, looming high,
Tempt our souls with whispered sighs.

What lies beyond, we dare to seek,
A world of wonder, strong yet weak,
Strength found in the shadows' hold,
Stories waiting to be told.

Fear and courage intertwined,
In the depths, our truths we find,
Crossing thresholds of despair,
Hope ignites in fragrant air.

Step through the wards of night so deep,
Where ancient guardians chance to sleep,
Beyond the gates, a brighter fate,
Awaits the heart, a treasured state.

The Lost Echo of Memory

In halls of silence, shadows creep,
Whispers linger, dreams we keep.
Fragments of laughter, faded light,
Echoes of love in the quiet night.

Time steals moments, leaves us bare,
Fleeting glimpses of what was there.
A photograph worn, edges torn,
Faces we cherished, now forlorn.

Memory dances, never stays,
Fleeting like mist in morning rays.
Yet in the heart, they softly stir,
The lost echoes, a gentle blur.

A Passage to Nowhere

A winding road with endless turns,
Where every lantern slowly burns.
Footsteps fading into the night,
Dreams dissolve in the fading light.

The compass spins, the map unfolds,
Stories untold in whispers bold.
Each step a question, no reply,
Searching for answers beneath the sky.

In every shadow, doubts may grow,
Yet still we wander, hearts aglow.
Though paths may twist, and visions blur,
A passage to nowhere, yet we stir.

Flight Over Fabled Landscapes

Above the clouds, where eagles soar,
Landscapes shimmer, legends galore.
Mountains high with secrets old,
Rivers whisper tales untold.

Fields of gold and skies so blue,
Wonders bloom in every hue.
In the breeze, a song of lore,
A flight to dream, forevermore.

Chasing horizons, we break free,
In the heart of nature's spree.
Every glance uncovers grace,
Fabled lands in endless space.

The Forgotten Tales of Tomorrow

In pages worn, where dreams are sown,
Tales forgotten, seeds are thrown.
Visions of futures, bright and near,
Yet lost in silence, few will hear.

Echoes of laughter, hopes in flight,
Characters woven in time's gentle light.
Each story waits for the dawn's embrace,
A gentle whisper in time's vast space.

Tomorrow's promise, a fleeting glance,
In shadowed corners, chance and dance.
We pen the tales, though some may fade,
In every heart, new dreams are laid.

The Call of the Endless Green

In forests deep, where shadows play,
The whispering leaves invite my stay.
Among the ferns, a hidden trail,
Where nature's breath begins to sail.

A brook that sings with gentle tone,
Invites the heart to feel at home.
Green canopies that sway and dance,
Awake the spirit in a trance.

In every nook, a secret waits,
With blooming life that celebrates.
The mossy floors, the vibrant hues,
Nature's song, forever ensues.

The call of green, a timeless plea,
A world where souls can roam and be.
In endless realms of light and shade,
The heart finds peace, beneath the glade.

Reflections in a Crystal Lake

Beneath the sky, in still embrace,
A crystal lake, a timeless space.
It mirrors dreams, both near and far,
With every ripple, a shining star.

The trees lean close, to share their tales,
As twilight whispers in the gales.
Each drop of water holds the light,
Of fleeting moments, pure and bright.

In tranquil depths, my thoughts take flight,
Among the colors, day turns night.
A silken peace, a gentle sway,
In nature's arms, I drift away.

Reflections dance, a soothing balm,
Embracing silence, sweet and calm.
The lake, a canvas, vast and grand,
Invites my heart to understand.

Where the Sun Meets the Moon

At dawn's first blush, the skies unfold,
Where day and night in dance behold.
The sun awakes with golden rays,
While silver glimmers softly plays.

They share a wink, a fleeting glance,
In painted clouds, they weave a trance.
The horizon blushes, shadows flee,
In twilight's hues, they learn to be.

As day surrenders, stars ignite,
While whispers of the moon take flight.
Together they create a scene,
A love that's felt, yet seldom seen.

Where sun meets moon, a promise glows,
In dusk and dawn, their beauty flows.
From morn to eve, in symphony,
A dance of light, eternally.

A World of Awakened Fantasies

In hidden realms where dreams reside,
Where fantasies and hopes collide.
A tapestry of whispered sighs,
Where magic weaves beyond the skies.

With every thought, a door swings wide,
To lands where time and space abide.
The creatures of the night arise,
With twinkling lights in darkened skies.

Through forests bright and oceans deep,
The secrets of the heart we keep.
In every turn, a tale unfolds,
Adventures waiting to be told.

A world alive with vibrant hues,
Where dreams take flight, and joy imbues.
In this embrace of endless glee,
Awakened hearts forever free.

The Secrets of the Emerald Depths

In waters deep where shadows creep,
The emerald hues hold secrets steep.
Silent whispers call and sway,
Inviting souls to drift away.

Life dances in a liquid trance,
Where ancient fish in shadows prance.
The waves conceal what eyes can't see,
In depths where time can cease to be.

Secrets murmur in the flow,
Codes of silence, ebb and glow.
A coral palace, bright, alive,
A hidden world where dreams survive.

With every splash, a tale unfolds,
Of sunken ships and treasures bold.
The emerald depths, a mystic charm,
Ensnaring hearts with nature's calm.

A Breath of Forgotten Fire

In embers soft, where ashes lay,
A breath of fire stirs the gray.
Flickering flames that dance and sigh,
Unleashing dreams that long to fly.

Through whispered winds, the tales ignite,
Of passions lost and visions bright.
Each spark a memory, fierce and grand,
Lighting the dark with a gentle hand.

In shadows cast, old legends rise,
A symphony beneath the skies.
The warmth of hearth, the glow of kin,
Awakens souls that dwell within.

A breath of fire that once was lost,
Rekindled now, despite the cost.
In every flicker, hope is found,
Resilient spirit, burning sound.

Whispers of the Unseen

In twilight's veil, where senses tease,
The whispers float upon the breeze.
Ghostly echoes of what once was,
Speak secrets softly without a pause.

The unseen worlds weave in and out,
With shadows dancing, casting doubt.
Through hush of night, the stories call,
Entwined in silence, they enthrall.

In every rustle, a voice may stir,
Phantom stories wrapped in blur.
A glimpse of fate, a thread astray,
In this soft hush, we long to stay.

As moonlight bathes the earth so pure,
The unseen whispers, we endure.
Holding close what cannot show,
The heart's deepest secrets, softly flow.

Echoes from the Outer Realm

Beyond the stars, where dreams converge,
Echoes linger, soft and urge.
Voices of ages, distant, clear,
Calling forth what we hold dear.

In cosmic dance, the worlds align,
An astral lullaby, divine.
The outer realm, a magic place,
Where time dissolves, and spirits grace.

Through darkened voids, a gentle song,
Reminds us where we all belong.
Colors swirl in endless flight,
Illuminating the vast night.

Echoes resonate, guide our way,
A journey marked by starlit play.
In silence born from ancient hues,
We find our truths and fleeting views.

Echoing Songs of Lost Wanderers

In shadows deep, their voices weave,
A tale of paths that none believe.
Echoes linger, bittersweet,
In every heart, a restless beat.

Through moonlit nights and sunlit days,
They wander on in tireless ways.
With every step, a memory calls,
Of uncharted lands and ancient walls.

In whispers soft, they share their dreams,
Of rivers wide and silver streams.
Silent forests, towering high,
Where secrets dwell beneath the sky.

Yet paths may twist and shadows blend,
The stories bend, but never end.
For lost wanderers roam and sing,
With every echo, hope takes wing.

Between the Veils of Reality

In twilight realms where shadows play,
The line of dreams and truth is gray.
Between the veils, the whispers flow,
Of worlds unseen that softly glow.

Illusions dance on weary minds,
Where time unwinds and fate unwinds.
In every look, a tale concealed,
Of love and loss, the heart revealed.

Through veils of mist, visions steal,
The fabric of what we can feel.
A tapestry of stars and sighs,
In hidden realms where magic lies.

Yet as we search, the truth will fade,
In shadows cast, the dreams we've made.
Between those lines, we'll find our place,
In every heartbeat, a trace of grace.

Journeys to the Fabled Wilds

Beyond the hills where legends dwell,
A call to those who hear the bell.
Journeys beckon, wild and free,
To lands where dreams and courage be.

In forests deep and mountains high,
Where eagles soar and spirits fly.
The fabled wilds await our quest,
In nature's heart, we find our rest.

Through rivers swift and valleys low,
The seeds of wonder start to grow.
With every step, the magic grows,
In every breath, the wildness flows.

As stars align in endless skies,
We'll chase the sun, where freedom lies.
In fabled wilds, we forge our fate,
The journey calls, we will not wait.

Mysteries of the Floating Isles

Above the clouds where dreams take flight,
The floating isles in soft twilight.
Mysteries rise from shadows deep,
In whispers soft, the secrets keep.

With winds that sing of tales untold,
The islands shine in hues of gold.
A dance of light on waters clear,
With every chime, the past draws near.

In gardens lush, where visions bloom,
The essence of magic fills the room.
Through every breeze, a soft caress,
Inviting souls to seek and guess.

Yet every isle holds ancient lore,
Of hopes and dreams that we explore.
In mysteries vast, we find our thread,
As floating whispers call ahead.

Chronicles of the Starbound Dreamers

Under the starry skies we roam,
Chasing dreams, far from home.
Whispers of galaxies call our name,
In the dance of the cosmic flame.

Hearts ablaze with celestial light,
Guided by the moon's soft flight.
Each heartbeat echoes through the night,
As wanderers seek a brighter sight.

In the silence, stories unfold,
Of brave souls and fates bold.
Navigating the vast unknown,
In the symphony of stardust grown.

Together we carve our destiny,
In the tapestry of infinity.
Bound by hope, forever we soar,
Chronicles written on the astral shore.

The Garden of Forgotten Gods

In a meadow where silence reigns,
Ancient whispers linger like chains.
Forgotten gods in shadow play,
Watching over night and day.

Petals fall from timeless blooms,
Infused with tales of ancient glooms.
Roots entwined in myth's embrace,
Echoes of a lost, sacred space.

Figures carved in shadowed trees,
Offer secrets to the breeze.
Each echo a soft, gentle sigh,
Of deities that live nearby.

In this garden of fading light,
Hope flickers softly, burning bright.
For every tale that fades away,
A new one blossoms in its sway.

Flights of Fancy Over Silent Seas

On velvet wings the dreams take flight,
Over oceans kissed by night.
Waves whisper tales of distant lands,
In the twilight's gentle hands.

Clouds dressed in silver and gold,
Guard secrets that the seas hold.
Chasing horizons, we set sail,
In the embrace of the moonlit veil.

The winds carry laughter and tears,
Across the vast, silent frontiers.
Each gust a message from afar,
Guiding hearts like a wandering star.

In the twilight's tender grace,
We find magic in each traced space.
These flights of fancy weave and spin,
Across the seas, our dreams begin.

Lullabies of the Wandering Wind

Softly hums the evening breeze,
Carrying whispers through the trees.
Lullabies woven, gentle and sweet,
Swaying the world in rhythmic beat.

As shadows dance beneath the moon,
Nature's chorus sings a tune.
Stars blink softly with each sigh,
Guiding the night as dreams flutter by.

The wind carries stories untold,
Of distant lands where hearts are bold.
Each note a promise, pure and bright,
Lifting spirits into the night.

In the arms of the gentle fawn,
Dreamers rest till the light of dawn.
For every lullaby the wind spins,
A new adventure quietly begins.

Dawn Over the Lost City

Golden light spills wide,
Awakening the stone,
Whispers of the ancients,
Call the lost back home.

Shadows flee like dreams,
As rivers softly gleam,
A breath of hope unfolds,
In the dawn's warm beam.

Crumbled walls stand proud,
Echoes of the past,
In the silent ruins,
Stories that hold fast.

Birds lift their soft wings,
Singing tunes of old,
As the city stirs now,
In the morning gold.

Fables of the Endless Landscape

Across the rolling hills,
Whispers of the breeze,
Tales of sunlit valleys,
Where the heart can seize.

Mountains wear their crowns,
In the fading light,
Guardians of secrets,
In the hush of night.

Fields of emerald sway,
Under skies so wide,
Each blade a story,
In the world's great stride.

Rivers weave their paths,
Through a land of many,
Fables written soft,
In the heart's own pen.

Beyond Maps and Signposts

Where the compass spins wild,
And the stars can't guide,
Journey calls the brave,
To seek the unknown tide.

Through forests thick with time,
And mountains steep and high,
The spirit finds its way,
In the boundless sky.

Every step a moment,
Every turn a chance,
Lost in wonder's grasp,
Embraced by nature's dance.

Beyond the marked trails,
Lies the heart of true quest,
For in the wild's embrace,
We discover our best.

The Undying Quest

In the silence of night,
Stars blaze with fierce might,
Chasing shadows of doubt,
With a heart pure and bright.

Through trials and through tears,
Strengthened by our fears,
Each step a new chapter,
In the story of years.

Voices echo in dreams,
Of those who have strayed,
Lighting paths for the lost,
In the dusk's cool shade.

For the quest never ends,
With each dawn we rise,
Seeking truth in the world,
Beneath endless skies.

Portals to Infinity

In the depths of night, stars align,
Whispers cascade through space and time.
Fragments of dreams, they intertwine,
Opening paths where shadows climb.

Waves of the cosmos in silent dance,
Fleeting glimpses of a timeless chance.
Lost in wonder, we take a stance,
Chasing echoes in a cosmic trance.

Voices of ages call from afar,
Guiding us under the same bright star.
Together we wander, no need to spar,
Through these portals, we deeply spar.

In the end, we see, paths untold,
Through galaxies deep and worlds of gold.
With open hearts, stories unfold,
Portals to infinity, brave and bold.

The Beyond's Heartbeat

Listen close to the heartbeat, faint,
Echoing softly, a celestial saint.
In shadows deep, where whispers paint,
The tales of love, a cosmic restraint.

Holding dreams in the palm of night,
The beyond's call, a shimmering light.
With every pulse, the future ignites,
A dance of spirits in flight.

Moments linger like dew on grass,
Each heartbeat a wish, as memories pass.
In the silence where echoes amass,
The beyond's heartbeat, none can surpass.

United we stand at the edge of time,
Feeling the rhythm, our hearts align.
In wondrous realms, our souls combine,
The beyond's heartbeat, pure and sublime.

Gateway to the Dreamt Horizon

Open wide, the gateway glows,
Curves like rivers, where magic flows.
Step not lightly, as the wind knows,
A realm awakened, destiny shows.

Colors swirling, the canvas vast,
Where dreams are woven, shadows cast.
In whispers sweet, the future's past,
A dance of time that holds us fast.

Glimmers of hope through clouds appear,
Guiding the lost, silencing fear.
Onward we travel, with vision clear,
To the dreamt horizon, ever near.

In each heartbeat, adventure calls,
Through the doorway where magic falls.
Beyond horizons, the spirit enthralls,
Gateway to dreams, where love befalls.

Legacies of the Celestial Tide

The moon whispers secrets to the sea,
A tapestry woven in harmony.
Legacies borne on waves so free,
Guiding sailors to what shall be.

Stars sparkle like stories untold,
In the fabric of night, they unfold.
With each rise, the tales of old,
Celestial tides in their grasp, behold.

Bound by the pull of the universe high,
Dreamers drift gently beneath the sky.
In each motion, the voices sigh,
Legacies echoing back to the nigh.

Together we sail on this endless ride,
With hope in our hearts, where worlds collide.
Through the cosmos, our spirits slide,
In the legacies of the celestial tide.

Secrets Beneath Celestial Skies

Beneath the stars we whisper low,
The secrets that the night can show.
Moonlight dances on the sea,
Unveiling dreams, wild and free.

In shadows deep, the wonders lie,
Wrapped in veils of midnight sky.
With every twinkle, stories weave,
Of ancient hopes we dare believe.

The winds, they carry tales untold,
Of lovers lost and dreams of gold.
In silence, truth begins to bloom,
Under the watch of night's soft loom.

Each star a guardian, bright and bold,
Holding secrets the heart can hold.
In the serene embrace of night,
We find our path, guided by light.

The Realm Where Time Stands Still

In a place where moments pause,
Time falters, as the heart draws.
Each breath a whisper, soft and light,
Infinite stillness cloaks the night.

Echoes linger, sweet and slow,
Bathed in warmth of twilight glow.
Memories dance like fading stars,
Cradled close beneath the scars.

In this realm, lost dreams unify,
Each tear we shed, a reason why.
With every heartbeat, we ascend,
To find a space where pain can mend.

Here in the silence, souls align,
Bound by fate, your hand in mine.
Forever held in tender grace,
Time's embrace, our sacred space.

Pathways to the Unseen Valley

On the horizon where shadows play,
Lie hidden trails that lead away.
Through veils of mist and whispers low,
The unseen valley calls us so.

With leaves of emerald, paths unfold,
Secrets whisper, legends told.
Each step a journey, wild and bright,
To realms of wonder, pure delight.

The breeze carries scents of the past,
Memories linger, shadows cast.
As twilight falls, the world ignites,
With hues of dreams, our hearts take flight.

In the valley deep, we find our way,
Guided by hope to a brand new day.
With every heartbeat, magic brews,
In pathways paved with morning dew.

Enigmas of the Starlit Expanse

In the stillness, the cosmos breathes,
Mysterious patterns in twilight's wreaths.
Stars align, a cryptic dance,
We gaze in wonder, caught in trance.

Forgotten worlds begin to stir,
Whispers of dusk in every blur.
Galaxies spin with tales to share,
In the vastness, a cosmic affair.

Every twinkling light, a distant song,
Singing stories of where we belong.
In the silence, our spirits roam,
Finding in darkness, a sense of home.

The night sky holds such endless grace,
In starlit whispers, we find our place.
Enigmas linger, waiting to be,
Unraveled by love's infinity.

The Uncharted Narratives

In shadowed maps where dreams reside,
Whispers hint at paths to stride.
Each line a tale from ages past,
In ink and dusk, our memories cast.

Through trials etched on weathered skin,
Stories linger, where we begin.
Every heartbeat, every breath,
Marks journeys taken, dances with death.

Beyond the stars, in silent night,
Unwritten songs take wing in flight.
In every soul, a voice concealed,
A truth awaiting to be revealed.

From every corner, tales emerge,
Through valleys deep, and oceans surge.
With every word, we shape the fate,
And carve our names in time's debate.

Echoes of Forgotten Legends

In twilight's glow, the shadows weave,
Legends drift, and hearts believe.
Whispers rise from ancient stone,
And in their depths, we find our own.

Fables told in hushed refrain,
Of battles fought and love's sweet pain.
Resilience wrapped in tales of yore,
A dance of spirits on forgotten shore.

Through misty fields where silence reigns,
The past unfolds in gentle strains.
Echoes linger, soft yet clear,
Reminders that our roots are near.

With every sigh, the stories wake,
Speaking truths we long to take.
To honor those who came before,
As we pen tales forevermore.

The Gaze of the Infinite Horizon

Where earth and sky in whispers meet,
The horizon stretches, bittersweet.
A canvas brushed in hues of gold,
Hear the secrets that time unrolled.

With every dawn, a promise blooms,
As daylight chases away the glooms.
In every sunset, colors meld,
A fleeting glimpse of dreams upheld.

To look beyond what eyes can see,
Is to dance with fate, wild and free.
Each glance reflects our deepest fears,
Yet beckons hope through laughter and tears.

In stillness rests the boundless dream,
Where possibilities softly gleam.
To stare afresh at what's unknown,
Is to find the strength we've always grown.

Stories Carried by the Wind

Gentle breezes whisper tales,
Of distant lands and fading trails.
Through swaying trees and rustling leaves,
The wind unveils what the heart believes.

With every gust, memories soar,
From mountain peaks to ocean shore.
Wrapped in warmth, the echoes blend,
As nature's voice begins to mend.

Voices dance on currents high,
Each story floats, like birds in the sky.
To listen close, to hear the strain,
Of journeys lost and love regained.

A tapestry spun from the air,
Weaving lives in every layer.
The wind, a scribe of time and fate,
Cuts through silence, and resonates.

Beyond the Fractured Skies

Stars whisper secrets, softly they glow,
Through shattered heavens, where wild dreams flow.
Shadows of hope dance on the cold ground,
In twilight's embrace, solace is found.

Winds carry whispers, of journeys untold,
As night draws its curtain, the cosmos unfolds.
Each breath of stardust, a story of grace,
Beyond the fractured skies, we find our place.

Galaxies beckon, like eyes in the dark,
Illuminating paths where our spirits embark.
With each fleeting moment, we reach for the light,
Transforming despair into shimmering sight.

In the vastness of silence, our hearts learn to sing,
Bearing the weight of the hopes we bring.
Beyond every fracture, the beauty we see,
A tapestry woven of what strives to be.

Riddles of the Cosmic Sea

Waves of the cosmos, a dance of the night,
Stars twinkle in rhythm, a wondrous delight.
In the depths of the void, secrets entangle,
Riddles of time, like threads that dangle.

Nebulas shimmer, with colors so vast,
Holding the memories of futures and past.
Each quasar a whisper, each black hole a sigh,
In the cosmic ocean where dreams drift and fly.

Lighthouses of starlight guide sailors unbound,
Across the dark waters where mysteries abound.
With every new dawn, horizons extend,
Riddles unravel, as journeys blend.

The waves of infinity pull us along,
Voices of galaxies in a celestial song.
In this cosmic sea, we seek and explore,
Unraveling riddles, forevermore.

The Pioneers of the Unknown

With courage ignited, hearts filled with fire,
Pioneers of the unknown, they rise ever higher.
Through treacherous terrain, and shadows that loom,
They venture forth boldly, dispelling the gloom.

Charting new worlds with stars as their guide,
In the depths of the night, fear casts aside.
With eyes full of wonder, they pierce through the mist,
Embracing the magic that life can't resist.

Each step is a lesson, each stumble a chance,
In the dance of the cosmos, we learn to advance.
Together we journey, hand in hand, we create,
The story of all, weaving fate with our fate.

To seek the horizons where no one has been,
The pioneers rise where the light has not seen.
In the silence of space, their dreams take their flight,
Chasing the unknown, forging paths in the night.

Reflections of the Infinite Journey

Mirrors of time, reflecting our dreams,
In the heart of the cosmos, nothing is as it seems.
Footprints of stardust across galaxies roam,
Each spark a reminder, we're never alone.

As we wander the pathways where wonders unroll,
The infinite journey sings deep in the soul.
Through trials we venture and days we explore,
Each moment a treasure, a piece to restore.

Reflected in echoes of laughter and tears,
The tapestry woven from countless years.
In every connection, a universe grows,
In the dance of existence, the truth gently flows.

With each dawn that rises, our spirits ignite,
Illuminated pathways of soft morning light.
In the journey of life, as we follow our dreams,
Reflections of infinity flow in our streams.

Journey to the Forgotten Shore

The waves whisper soft secrets,
As we walk on the golden sand.
Footprints fade in the cool breeze,
Time slips like grains from the hand.

Shells adorned with stories old,
Glimmer beneath the sun's warm rays.
We gather memories like treasures,
A journey marked by countless days.

Seagulls dance on the horizon,
Their cries echo through the blue sky.
Every step takes us further,
To places where dreams learn to fly.

The shore greets us with open arms,
Each tide brings a chance to explore.
In this realm of endless wonder,
We find what we've searched for before.

Shadows of a Distant Horizon

Beneath a sky painted with gold,
Shadows stretch and softly sway.
Whispers of night begin to unfold,
As the sun bids farewell to day.

A path twists through the silent trees,
Where secrets linger in the air.
Every rustle holds a mystery,
In twilight's charm, we wander there.

Figures shift like fleeting dreams,
Amongst the whispers of the night.
Echoes dance on moonlit beams,
Chasing shadows, we find our light.

Each step takes us further still,
Into the heart of twilight's song.
In shadows of the distant hill,
We find where we've always belonged.

The Secret Beyond the Veil

In the quiet of a hidden grove,
Mysteries weave through the air.
A curtain of mist softly hovers,
Guarding secrets beyond compare.

Leaves whisper tales of ancient lore,
As the wind carries stories anew.
Each branch holds an unseen door,
Inviting wanderers like me and you.

What lies beyond in the silent night?
Curiosity sparks every heart.
With open minds and hopeful light,
We crave the magic that sets us apart.

Through the veil, we shall venture deep,
Where shadows twine with golden dreams.
In this realm, our souls may leap,
To uncover the truth of our schemes.

Paths Through the Twilight

A winding path beneath the stars,
Leads to a realm where time stands still.
Each step echoes with whispered hearts,
In twilight's embrace, we gather will.

The sky, a canvas of dreams unfurled,
Bathed in hues of deep purple and blue.
We stroll through the magic of this world,
Hand in hand, with visions anew.

In shadows cast by the bending trees,
We find our way through the night.
Every breath a gentle breeze,
Guiding us deeper in soft twilight.

Together, we tread this sacred ground,
With stars as our guiding light.
Through the paths that know no bounds,
We journey on with hearts so bright.

Reveries of the Starlit Valleys

In valleys deep, where shadows play,
The whispers of the night hold sway.
Stars twinkle bright, a silver hue,
Dreams awaken, nothing feels new.

The cool breeze sings a gentle tune,
Guiding hearts beneath the moon.
Where silence reigns, and thoughts can soar,
In reveries, we seek for more.

With every step on sacred ground,
The magic stirs without a sound.
Each glimmer speaks of what has passed,
In starlit valleys, forever vast.

So let us wander, hand in hand,
In dreams that weave a mystic strand.
For in these depths, our spirits free,
In starlit valleys, we shall be.

Whispers from the Unknown Canopy

In shadows cast by emerald leaves,
A symphony of silence weaves.
The unknown calls, a gentle sigh,
Beneath these boughs, our spirits fly.

Every rustle, a tale untold,
Secrets wrapped in shades of gold.
The canopy holds dreams and fears,
In whispered tones, the world appears.

Weaving light through branches high,
A dance of shadows in the sky.
With every breath, we commune deep,
In the unknown, we dare to leap.

The heart beats strong, the mind will roam,
Among the whispers, we find home.
In nature's arms, we find our way,
Beneath the canopy, we stay.

The Serenade of Unseen Wonders

In the twilight's gentle embrace,
Unseen wonders find their place.
A serenade drifts through the air,
Magic lives in every layer.

Where shadows bloom and colors blend,
In silence, we begin to mend.
The night's song calls to every heart,
In unseen realms, we play our part.

With every note, the universe glows,
Revealing paths where river flows.
Each star a wonder, bright and clear,
In the song of nights, we draw near.

So close your eyes, let feelings sway,
To the serenade of night and day.
In every breath, a magic found,
In unseen wonders, we are bound.

The Light Beneath the Unknown

In deep of night, the shadows creep,
A beacon glows where secrets sleep.
The light beneath the unknown calls,
Echoes softly as darkness falls.

It dances lightly on the streams,
Illuminating quiet dreams.
In the stillness, it will guide,
Through the veils where fears reside.

Each flicker tells a story vast,
Of futures held and the past.
The radiance breaks the chains of doubt,
In every heart, it blooms throughout.

So step with faith into the night,
For there awaits that tender light.
In what is hidden, truth will be shown,
The light beneath the unknown is our own.

Journeys Through Celestial Labyrinths

Amidst the stars, the path unfolds,
With cosmic maps and stories told.
Through swirling lights and shadows deep,
We wander on, our dreams to keep.

A comet's tail, a galaxy's spin,
We chart the paths where wonders begin.
In nebulae, our hopes ignite,
Guided by the endless night.

The Milky Way, a gentle stream,
Its silken waves, a glowing dream.
We sail through realms of endless space,
In search of truth, we find our place.

Each heartbeat echoes, cosmic sound,
As stardust whispers, love unbound.
Through labyrinths of time we glide,
In celestial arms, forever reside.

The Whispering Woods of Mystery

In twilight's grasp, the woods alive,
Where secrets dwell and shadows thrive.
Beneath the boughs of ancient trees,
The whispers dance upon the breeze.

Each rustle tells a tale unspun,
Of moonlit nights and forgotten sun.
The owls call out in muffled flight,
Guardians of the spectral night.

Paths weave like dreams in hazy mist,
A world concealed in nature's tryst.
Through thickets thick and foliage bright,
We wander deep, in search of light.

With every step, the stories grow,
In harmony with winds that blow.
The whispering woods, forever near,
With every breath, the magic's clear.

Hymns from the Exiled Haven

In shadows cast by distant skies,
We sing our hymns, where silence lies.
The echoes of a lost embrace,
Resound within this sacred space.

From exile's heart, our voices rise,
A symphony of unseen ties.
Each note a plea, each word a dream,
In the stillness, hope's soft gleam.

We gather strength from stories shared,
In whispered tales, the heart laid bare.
Fractured souls in unity,
Create a bond, a harmony.

The haven's light, a flickering flame,
Illuminates our hopes, our name.
In every hymn, a promise sent,
From exiled hearts, a love content.

The Horizon's Veiled Secret

At dawn's first blush, the world awakes,
With golden hues, the silence breaks.
A ribbon stretched 'neath skies so vast,
The horizon holds its secrets cast.

In twilight's glow, the shadows play,
Painting dreams along the way.
What lies beyond that distant bend?
A mystery with no true end.

The waves embrace the sandy shore,
Each crest a tale, a whispered lore.
The sun descends, the stars ignite,
Guiding hearts into the night.

As we chase the fading light,
We ponder what is out of sight.
For in each step, in every breath,
Lies the beauty woven with depth.

Milton Keynes UK
Ingram Content Group UK Ltd.
UKHW022050111124
451035UK00014B/1042